before we break

KILA CHAN

Contents

Preface

While your journey of growth can only be experienced by you alone, I am here to remind you that you do not have to feel alone. Even when you fall and it feels like you have been broken into pieces, I want you to remember before you break that you are more resilient than you think. You might find yourself wandering in the dark for miles, feeling stuck in the same place, or hitting a wall wherever you turn. And the daunting part of all of this is that things could stay this way for a long time, especially if you are unsure of how to move forward. But even then, nothing can inhibit you from rising toward the light that is your truth. What it takes to get there resides in you, even if it means having to claw your way out and getting a few scrapes along the way.

I wrote these words for myself because there were many times when I struggled with the way I felt in my own relationships and did not know where to turn for clarity, other than toward my journals that have been receptive to just about every feeling I would have rather preferred to repress. My journals have been integral to my existence, and it was in writing about these struggles that I realized how detrimental I was toward myself. It seemed like I was primarily at the root of most of my issues, as they stemmed from how I operated and how I thought the world around me should operate. Whenever things deviated from my viewpoint, all I saw were problems—

and becoming aware of this made it quite unsettling to live with myself.

Writing these words that you are about to read was like embarking on a journey of bittersweet self-discovery. This journey put a spotlight on my most vulnerable moments and exposed the parts that I did not love about myself. The more I discovered, the more alone I felt. But I had to get past that. That fear of feeling like I was the only one going through what I was going through. Because I know I am not alone. So, although I had written these words for my own peace of mind, I especially put this book together for you because perhaps you can relate.

Perhaps you know what it is like to have to sit with your pain and not know how to navigate through it. To have experienced the parts of love that initially felt great but ended up hurting you instead and made you afraid to find joy again. But perhaps you also know what it is like to believe in your worth enough to do the hard things. To go to great lengths to protect your peace the moment you find it again.

Whenever you find yourself at a dead end or just not where you thought you would be, I hope you have self-compassion. I hope these words will be a source of light on the path that leads you back to yourself.

Kila Chan

The Fall

Sorry Doesn't Cut It

We crave apologies the way a disgruntled sweet tooth craves sugar, believing that receiving an apology would magically soothe us. Maybe we were conditioned to demand it, because that meant we could finally let go of the hurt. But those of us who have ever received a full-fledged apology know that it is completely meaningless unless followed by changed behavior. We do not need the repeated, "I'm sorry I hurt you." The glorified *sorry* does not equate to change. It could never be enough for us to thrive on, yet we have conditioned ourselves to let it be enough.

Seed

I was ignorant and presumed that you would always be by my side. I planted this expectation into my heart like a seed in soil and obsessively tended to it. I watered it the way one might when several days in a row were missed or when they suddenly remembered that the plant existed and was already wilting. I thought that I could keep you from leaving. I tried every which way to make you stay, but suffocating you was not the solution. It was only after you left my side that I realized the plant I was trying so hard to keep alive had long been drowned from my overwatering.

Never Ready

When people fail you, they do not consider what that does to you. They say sorry like they mean it, and they probably do, but the apology extends far enough to cover only their own tracks. Their apology is just enough to get themselves out of trouble. They do not realize that this is not your first rodeo—that others have failed you before. And they will continue to leave you in disappointment because even your most marginal expectations of them may be too much for them to fulfill. Some people will never be ready to give you what you need.

Waiting

We were taught the value of having patience from our days of youth. We learned that our ability to be patient determined how deserving we were of good things. It is no wonder, then, that we have conditioned ourselves to wait for change promised by those who continually abuse their chances. We end up believing the hollow vows to be better and to do differently because the change we hope to see is the good thing we feel we deserve. "Don't hold your breath," they say, but we continue waiting for change that may never happen. And all we can hope for is that our lungs have the capacity.

Choosing

I wish that when people chose to leave us, we could choose not to miss them afterward. But the Universe tends to have a say in all that concerns us, and sometimes, it seems to conspire with our hearts against our heads, forbidding us from having our way.

Heart Wounds

We have a habit of overlooking the wounds we trust will heal simply with time. Similarly, we think that time is all we need for heartache to subside, but the passage of time alone will never be enough to take away the kind of hurt we are often left with. We will think we have healed, but soon after that, we will continue allowing into our lives the same people who are prone to reintroduce the very pain we had never actually overcome. Wounds of the heart may close up over time, but because they are often left unattended in their healing, they are only bound to reopen sooner or later.

Patches

Maybe one day we will learn to love ourselves better—
wholeheartedly, without skimping on quality. But for now, we
will love ourselves in the ways they have shown us: in patches,
when it is convenient, and when we feel like it.

Hooked

They tell us affectionate things to reel us in, as if we were fish about to bite. And maybe we will be enticed enough to take the bait and start to feel like we were special. But the difference between us and the fish is that once either of us is hooked, only one of us has the capacity to choose our next move. Only one of us can opt out of what comes next. And yet, we both will end up going down similar paths.

Home

Nobody warns us that the heart will make homes in places where it is not permanently wanted. It is tricked into thinking each place is forever, so it unpacks its belongings and gets comfortable—so comfortable that it would never be able to tell when it is no longer wanted. And when it is told to move out, it will not be ready for the pain. Eviction is not pretty, but neither are the hearts of those we thought would never hurt us.

Regret

Certain things we say will always roll off our tongues with instant regret. We blurt out things like, "Just tell me what is wrong with me," and, "When did you stop loving me?"— everything we desperately wish we did not want to know the answers to. Speaking up about what the heart wants is risking regret, but nothing provokes regret more than biting our tongues and letting what could be our last chance to change things slip away.

Winner

We never think that we can hurt other people. It is always them at fault. *They* are the inconsiderate ones. *They* cause all the pain. And *we* are always the victims who can do no wrong. They act selfishly some of the time, and still we will remember it for decades to come. We are convinced that if there had to be a comparison between whomever gets hurt more frequently, we would be the clear winners. And since we are so confident that we are more often on the receiving end of pain, it would seem self-defeating—hypocritical, really—for us to do the harming. The reality, though, is that we are equally capable of inflicting the same damage, but because we have trouble admitting to it, we can never call ourselves the real winners here.

Afterthought

When something is precious to you, you do your best to preserve it. Even on the days when it may feel like a chore. The effort does not stop just because you grow tired or busy. When it is meaningful enough, making sure it is taken care of should never be an afterthought, no matter how much of yourself is required to keep it functioning. It is the moment it becomes less than a priority that the need to maintain its top quality is lost. Failing to give it attention is stealing its ability to thrive. That is why we are what we are—inoperative and worn-out. Because things fall apart when they are not sustained. And even as we know this, we tell ourselves under our breath that not all things are designed to work forever.

Only Good Thing Left

They put us in a position that forbids us from choosing anything other than them. Some would call it toxic, but how could we differentiate what is toxic or not if it is all we have ever known? We are made to believe we could lose them in an instant if we ever chose ourselves. We are made to feel powerless, trapped in a loop of endlessly trying to please them, even if it means losing bits and pieces of who we are along the way. And we know we would be better off standing our ground and saying no to them, yet we choke up whenever we are close to finding our voice. With no luck, we eventually reduce ourselves to mush in a pitiful attempt to salvage whatever good is left. What we do not realize is that if there was any good left, surely, we were it.

Sweet and Sour

Love is sweet whenever my heart feels a slight ache without your presence. It is wanting to move closer to you even when you are already sitting next to me on the couch. I have known this kind of love and have tried holding on to it, but sometimes, things slip right through our hands the moment we loosen our grip. The moment we start to get more comfortable. A sweet love can go sour when we are hurt by the ones from whom we once never wanted to be apart. Love is sour when my heart aches in your presence. It is feeling lonely even when you are next to me on the couch.

I am left wondering how we got here.

Curse

Every time we give them a piece of our hearts and hope to receive a piece of theirs in return but are only left disheartened, we allow them to chip away at our self-worth. Sometimes we give our hearts to people who have grown comfortable reaping the benefits of our time and energy, while they expend as little of their own as possible and call it an attempt to meet us halfway. But instead of recognizing when we have given too much, we continue showing up, all the while cursing ourselves for not knowing the difference between what we deserve and our willingness to be at their disposal.

Begging

When you beg for attention, you are inviting vulnerability in.
Everything they do—if it is not to make you happy—makes you
feel "less than" in some way, and it becomes nearly impossible
for you to acknowledge the things they do for you. You begin to
compare how attentive they are toward others to how attentive
they are toward you, and the latter is always never enough. And
because you believe that to be the truth, you are often left
feeling insecure, even if they had no intention of causing you to
feel that way. When you beg for their attention, not only are you
forgetting your worth, but also that you should not have to beg
in the first place.

Deny

When you notice the red flags but simply knock them over, you deny your heart the honesty it deserves. You send your heart through waves of turmoil, but it has adapted to pain so well that it is unfazed by the consequences of what you choose not to face. Dodging the warning signs in the short term may not cause lasting damage, but refusing to ever confront what makes you uneasy just because it would hurt you to face the truth will only leave your heart tormented as all it will come to love is deception.

Promises

Promises are made to give us hope that change will happen eventually. We make promises on several occasions—after we mess up and hurt someone we love, amid panic, when we are happy, and especially after we have been forgiven. In hopes that they stay, we scramble to get our words right, pledging to do differently the next time around. If we are given another chance for redemption, we set out with hopeful hearts to deliver on our newly made promises—at least, that is what we nervously tell ourselves we will do. We all know that these promises are as long-lived as some of our New Year's resolutions that we were only slightly serious about when making them.

Searching

I have searched high and low. Dug deeply and rummaged through my entire being. Emptied out the contents of and scrutinized what might have been wrong with my heart. And still, I have yet to uncover the reasons you left. Instead, I am left again, but now with an emptied heart that still searches for the love that got away.

Hard Pill to Swallow

I have found only one other thing to be as true as change is the only constant in life, and it is this: When all is said and done, I cannot force anyone to do anything from places their heart is clearly not genuinely in. I could never make anyone love me, want me, or see me from a loving heart. It may be a hard pill to swallow, but if any of these must be forced, could I even call it love? The truth is I am fearful these places have been vacant all along, with their heart nowhere to be found. But I am not so keen to look inside to find out.

Alone

Why do we beg people not to go when they are already halfway out the door? No matter whose fault it is, they will somehow put a spin on things to make us feel like we had driven them away. Which is manipulative because we end up apologizing for things we may not have even done, and on top of that we beg them not to leave. All because we refuse to be the ones responsible for letting things end. All because we cannot face the truth that we do not know how to be alone. We reach for and cling to any part of them we can hold on to, but they see right through us and use it to their advantage. Knowing when to let things end is just as important as trying to salvage what is left, but we would rather lose our dignity any day than have to be alone.

Second Chance

You say change does not happen overnight, as if to reassure me that I should still expect it. But you insist it so often that it has become your mantra each time you are forgiven. The record was never broken—you have customized it to play that way. Your words are on repeat in my head: "Change does not happen overnight." But I would tell you that you are mistaken. It is not that it cannot happen over the course of one night. It only cannot happen if you choose not to allow it, and you have chosen not to allow it. Yet I will be the fool still hoping for the day to come, still handing out second chances to you like they were going out of style.

Choices

The bitter reality of deciding between two choices is that most of the time we cannot go back and elect the other option if things end up not working out with the first. When we choose one, we are also letting go of a different opportunity to be happy, and then whether we would be happier with that other opportunity would be impossible to know. The last thing we want to do is doubt ourselves, because in the end we would be living with the choice we made. And even if we reconsidered, we have to understand one thing: We could be the best thing to ever happen, but people do not wait around to find out. And if they did, then they would be the fools.

Repel

Many of us are too modest when measuring our own abilities, but when it comes to making questionable choices in love, it seems we hand ourselves the award. Maybe we subliminally view ourselves as hard to love because accepting that an easy love is attainable just seems out of range for us, and we are notorious for repelling any good thing that easily comes our way. When things consistently fail to work out as intended, we begin to think we are destined for unfortunate outcomes in everything we do, despite what we do. Even when something right comes along, we push it away to spare ourselves from the anticipated hurt.

We never realize that anticipating this hurt is what hurts us.

Point of No Return

We spew hurtful words at each other, thinking it will create an impact. As if they will hear us at last when it starts to sting. Like we will finally have their attention the moment our words resemble the bitter truth. We try to avoid reaching the point of no return because it is at this exact point where it would be too late to rescind our words. But why is it that they hear us only once we have said things that cannot be unsaid? Up until then, there was no room for remorse. We were only being honest, yet all we could do was stew in our guilt. Maybe there is no room for honesty without making each other feel awful at the same time.

Complacent

You wanted to know when things changed between us. They changed the moment we felt a sense of total complacency in our lives but reaching that level of comfort was not the problem. The problem was that you continued not to make the extra effort even after you were made aware of your minimal efforts. The problem was in the way you allowed me to carry the weight of our burdens alone, just because I chose to prioritize the things that I believed were important to us. When something matters to you, you take care of it. But your complacency showed me that even I was on that list of what did not matter to you.

Flower

We fell away from each other the way the last remaining petals of a wilting rose fall off. It is not easy to watch the bittersweet unraveling of something that so naturally formed together. Holding things together seemed almost effortless to do, but it only appeared that way from the outside, and it was only a matter of time before we would need to face the truth. We could not deny that our season of love had run its course, as we came to the realization that love alone will never be enough. Because even when they have everything they need to thrive, flowers eventually wither. Sometimes, we are like flowers.

Afloat

Even in the shallowest bodies of water our love could not stay afloat. Dilemmas with seemingly easy solutions became too dire. Every time you failed to keep your promises. Every time I made a minor mistake. Every time we did things without consideration for each other's feelings. We had a way of exaggerating the magnitude of any hurtful thing we did, and we were often so crushed by the weight of our actions that we no longer knew how to come up for air. We did not know how to help each other without submerging the other more. I desperately wanted to drain the water somehow, but the reality is we could never take away the water—we just had to learn how to stand in it.

Door

I catch myself staring at our front door longer than anyone should ever be staring at anything. Wondering at what moment it will swing open and you would walk in with the same apologetic look on your face that I have come to expect. Each passing hour is another hour spent in despair. Everything grows cold—the dinner, the air, my heart. It is nothing new, for this is what you do. And before I turn in, I spend the final moments of my waiting berating myself for being fooled yet again. It is nothing new, for this is what I do.

Nonsensical

We kick them out but not before making sure the key is under the doormat outside. We drive off, swearing never to return to them as we find ourselves already making that left turn to go back. We do the things that barely add up and label it "love." A love that has weathered a few beatings yet still sustained the resilience to heal. We continue this nonsensical give-and-take of love and pain because we cannot understand why we are not good enough for them to *want* to be what we need. But even when we ask them to release our hearts, we do not realize we are the very ones tightening their grip. No, we do not want them to return our hearts. We want to prove we are enough, and that, I am afraid, is what keeps us from moving forward. That is what keeps us from letting them let us go.

Blame Game

I blamed you for giving up on us. I made it clear that I was done, but only after deflecting the fault from me to you. What followed those words that relentlessly spilled out of my mouth was the most deafening silence. I knew then in my heart it was too late to retract any fingers I had pointed. Nothing could have made either of us feel better or worse. Not with you already feeling remorseful about your involvement in our pain, and not with me knowing that I had fully blamed you for our downfall that I was just as guilty of causing. And I had every reason to feel guilty because I expected the impossible, like for you to magically read my mind and somehow understand what I needed without me having to say a single word. This blame game could not have saved us, even if I had won.

The Past

I wonder about the past and whether we honestly move forward from it. If we never touch on the moments that have hurt us, does it mean we were able to let go of them? Or have we merely learned to meld the pain with our mundane lives and chosen to keep quiet about it? Memories can outwardly torment us and still remain buried within the walls of our minds. Surely, the past creeps up on us to serve as a reminder of something we need. A reminder of a pain with which we are familiar but had never been able to forget about or move on from. And maybe some sick part of us does not want to forget, because that would mean forgetting the harm people are capable of inflicting.

Empty

The goal was never to love so hard that we would exhaust ourselves. It was to love just enough so they could thrive on what we were giving them without making us feel like what we had to offer was not enough. Without making us feel like we owed it to them to prioritize their happiness over our own. When love is equally met from both ends, it should never be more troublesome than enjoyable to give of ourselves. We should not have to burn through our fuel to make them happy while their tanks remain full. But oftentimes, we are left running on empty.

Things They Never Tell Us

Those who teach us about love speak of it as if it is a piece of treasure and the only one worth hanging on to. Even after hearing of all the untold tragedies that stem from love, they still deduce that love is always worth getting back into the game for. Although they gently warn us of the possibility that along the way we may lose our sense of self, and maybe even our heart, they tend to omit the part where some of us never regain these things once they are gone and how such a loss can ultimately skew the lens through which we see ourselves. They never mention that some of us never become fully restored even after the wounds close. These are the things they never tell us.

Greetings

Some nights we greet our demons with a gentle hug. Not because we missed them or welcome their presence, but because they are what most closely resembles comfort in our lives. When all we have been relishing in is anything that provides comfort, it only makes sense that what we desperately need banished from our lives is the very thing we want to keep nearby. Nothing understands our damaged parts better than our sorrows. Our sorrows never try to make us feel guilty for staying put, for not being ready to move forward. Maybe we have learned to rely too heavily on our demons, given that we expect them to show up almost dutifully, ready to remind us of our pain if we were to ever forget. Is there a kindness to them? Perhaps in a painful but merciful and sympathizing sense, there is. So, we repay their kindness by making room for them.

White Flag

I was once told that any relationship I might find myself in next would give rise to the same issues I came across in my previous ones. It was their nice way of telling me that I was the problem and always would be. Naturally, these words were etched in my mind and would haunt me for years to come. And they did. Because even throughout my efforts to prove them wrong, I still managed to turn those unsettling words into reality each time I found myself trapped in the same debacle I thought I had finally learned to escape from. By the time I was ready to face the truth that I was the problem, I had already run off to my hiding place—wherever it was safe for me to wave a white flag at my insecurities. Wherever I could comfortably wallow in everything I did not want to believe but knew was wrong with me.

Conservation

I had never been wise about conserving my tears. I used up my supply at the most inappropriate times—moments when I felt badly hurt, but never badly enough to the point where the pain should necessitate tears. As if there were *right* moments to let them fall from my eyes, or *right* moments to get hurt. I reprimanded myself whenever I could not hold them back, even as they poured reflexively. But the tears were easy to brush off, knowing you were the source of my pain and that it was the only thing left that connected us.

Out of Line

When our reactions do not sit well with them, they say we are out of line. We are dismissed the moment we begin to sound like a broken record, which is the moment they stop hearing us altogether and call us crazy. But crazy is how we obsessively contemplate what we did to warrant such treatment. The way we wish over and over to take back whatever words and reactions started it all. The way we feel terribly about feeling terribly in the first place. What is out of line is that we choose to deal with them when they would rather not deal with us. It is choosing to continue tolerating those who ignore our broken hearts long before they have even had a chance to break.

Absurd

While feeling remorse is appropriate when the situation demands it, it is totally absurd when we have normalized feeling guilty for doing things that normally should not evoke guilt. But that is me—totally absurd. I thought that by truthfully addressing what hurts me I would be freeing myself of the uncomfortable emotions. But I would end up feeling invalidated instead as I would later find myself apologizing for how I was feeling. If I knew that my feelings mattered to you only when they were to your liking, I would rather disappoint you than feel slighted by you. I would rather remain unheard than know that you hear me only when I have good things to say. I would rather be disregarded at all times than act absurdly and reduce myself to being at your disposal. But that is me—totally absurd.

Foreign

When people try to communicate with us in languages we do not understand, their words are meaningless if we cannot grasp the translation. And maybe the language they speak is the only one they know, but without each other's help to understand, anything can easily be misread and taken the wrong way. It is no different in the language of love. In love, there will always be miscommunication when we fail to help each other receive love the way it is intended to be received. It is when we refuse to try to understand each other that love becomes foreign to the heart.

Power

Whenever we are faced with denying the people we care for, we find ourselves struggling to say no to them even when we may be screaming it in our heads. We have developed a habit of always making ourselves available for certain people because they are the ones we never want to let down. Our heads fill with harrowing thoughts of them leaving us if we failed to please them. We think that by not giving them what they want, they would no longer have use for us. When we hand them the power to control us, we lose control of our power.

Disgusted

By the time I realized that I could dictate how I wanted to be treated by others, my relationship with myself was already in jeopardy. I allowed myself to accept relationships with people that were no longer good for me, just because at one point they were. I chose to tolerate behaviors I was not okay with but had convinced myself were founded on love. There was nothing I could do about how other people chose to treat me, but that did not mean I needed to welcome it. I had accepted love in the form of convenience, and I was disgusted with myself for settling for it. When you believe that love works only on other people's terms, that misunderstanding will open the gates to only your own suffering.

Old Patterns

The greatest way to disrespect ourselves is by suppressing what the heart needs. Rather than listen when it tries to make apparent to us what we deserve, we silence it and let our habits take over. If given the choice, we will likely gravitate toward what feels familiar to us even when something about the familiar seems amiss. Easily, we stay with what we have known to work. But we would not be between choices if things were actually working out well. When we encounter something better suited for us but reject it because we fear the risk that things will change, we are choosing old patterns. Sometimes, we will choose wrong and force ourselves to believe we chose right.

Sabotage

I have heard stories of other people sabotaging their own opportunities for love, and at the time, it sounded laughable to me. But these days, I sympathize them because I know that those who turn away from love are the ones who can love with every ounce of their entire being but had simply been hurt and mishandled in the past. Maybe I am just a coward for giving up, but at least I am willing to admit it. Love might be well within reach, but my arms are tired from reaching for it to no avail. And I have heard the ending to this kind of story enough times to conclude that maybe I am not meant for love.

Imprisoned

To think that the people we love will never hurt us would be to live in a fairy tale. Eventually they will, even when we fully trust them not to, because what might be hurtful to us may not at all come across as hurtful to them, and it would be unfair of us to fault them for something so subjective. But what might be even more unfair is to expect that they will always find ways to hurt us. If all we did was constantly keep our guards up, we would be deluding ourselves into believing that the love they give us cannot be trusted. If we believe we are only bound to get betrayed, we will remain imprisoned by these expectations and that alone will do more damage to us than anyone we love ever could.

Discarded

I discarded what I originally had written here in the same way we discarded the life we had built together. But before giving up, I tried to salvage whatever I could, starting by analyzing every detail from the careless mistakes to the parts that were nothing short of remarkable, to going over what actually went wrong, and finally to figuring out the improvements that could be made. It dawned on me that maybe there was no way to make something better appear from what I had in front of me. That perhaps the only solution, unfortunately, was to start again. It would be easier to just leave things as they are, but that would mean turning a blind eye to the problems that desperately need resolving. If we do not address the problems before us and instead choose to settle for ways that we know deep down have never really worked, we will not know the better things that can emerge from starting over.

When Things are Toxic

There is no such thing as a toxic person, even if you feel like you may be with one, or that you are one yourself. When what was once a healthy environment you shared with someone is now exuding toxicity, the only option left—if the goal is to rectify anything—is to outgrow each other. Without first giving yourself the space to rediscover who you are individually and to make any necessary changes, you will forever be incapable of overlooking even their smallest mistake, let alone wiping their entire slate clean. Toxic people do not exist. There are only people with needs that are either constantly met or unmet. There are only people who try to force those needs to be met upon those who have lost the willingness to try altogether.

Window

I had gotten upset with you for presuming I would always be there, when I was the one who made it a point to stick around. I had shaken my head in disbelief at the way you had me at the bottom of your list of priorities when I was the one offering to be patient and wait my turn. Sometimes, we leave the window open and then complain when flies get in.

Rubber

I was so good at overextending myself, you would have thought I was made entirely of rubber. At least if I were made of rubber—as silly as it sounds—I would have felt no pain! But sadly, the pain reduced to a norm as I learned to grow numb to it in the same way you had grown numb to my needs. The only thing that hurt more than getting burned out trying to keep us functioning was that you were sitting back and watching me crumble.

Criminal

We back away, pretending things are fine to avoid the arguments. We hold our tongues when we would rather burn each other with uncalled-for words we both know will only start a fire. We sweep things under the rug and then go on with our day-to-day acting like everything is fine. Maybe we thought this act might save whatever was still untarnished after the last fire. But we knew at heart nothing could be spared that way—not with the damage that had already been done. We had confused what was real with what was ideal. It was criminal, and there was no way we could get away with acting like nothing between us was wrong.

The Rise

Gentle Waves

While hurting is essential for healing to follow, we cannot allow our suffering to dictate our lives. If we gave in to the pain, we would be losing a fair battle by default simply because we chose not to put up a fight. If we gave in to the pain, we would be losing ourselves to a love that may have ended but whose ending does not signify the end of the world. So, we must fight to revive our spirits; we must fight to heal the wounds in our hearts. And when we heal, we will not recognize it at first because healing comes in gentle waves. But we will know that we have healed when not even the most painful memory of them clenches the heart.

Bloom

A pained heart that has not fully healed will yield only distrust and pain. And they will grow like unwanted weeds that have been abandoned in our garden for so long that it would almost seem like we wanted them there. But if we give things around us a fair chance and trust ourselves to love again, we will see that our garden is more than these overgrown weeds, as we are more than our pain. We are the kindness we were never shown. The stability we hoped for but were never given. We are the sunlight peeking through the clouds after the rain. The flowers that still bloom despite all they have weathered.

Listen

Wherever I went, I ran into good old pain from my past, except the encounter would be less friendly and more like running into someone I have been trying to avoid. I had always been afraid, not of pain itself, but of what it would mean for me after we confronted each other. If I did not follow the right steps to ease my pain, would I always be shaken by it? We despise the hurt so much that our natural response is to get rid of it immediately, without spending a second more to think about its implications. I had never considered pain an indicator of anything other than a feeling I did not want to have, which is relative to what pain tries to tell us. It shows us certain things in life we might be better off without. It tells us what our hearts should be careful to avoid, and it would do us well to listen whenever our pain spoke.

Forgiveness

If you ever find yourself choosing between forgiveness and resentment, always choose forgiveness. People you trust not to hurt you will always find a way to do so, but it is not your job to counteract that or make sure that they refrain from hurting you. Bringing yourself to forgive is acknowledging that you have been hurt while also making it clear that you do not want to be controlled by that pain anymore. Although at first it may seem like you are absolving somebody of their guilt for their actions, choosing to forgive is ultimately something you are doing to set yourself free. It does not mean they have a place in your life again or that you owe it to them. In fact, they may not even deserve your forgiveness, but you deserve your peace.

Lightyears

We treat happiness as if it derived from a distant source—one that is outside of ourselves. Everybody wants us to find happiness, but they fail to reassure us that we do not need to look far or toward other people to find it. We forget to appreciate what we already have because we spend more time lamenting over the things we are missing—the things we believe we need to acquire to be content. Seeing that we constantly want more than what is in front of us and tend to look beyond wherever we are, happiness always seems lightyears away. We forget that fulfillment is found within, and the source we so fervently search for is the one doing the searching.

Exit

Sometimes, we hold on to something not necessarily because we still want it around, but because letting go of it would mean letting go of the way it made us feel. Feelings are what we hold dear, even long after their source has made an exit from our lives. And while it is okay to miss feeling a certain way, we are not obligated to keep something around simply because of what it did for us in the past. If it can no longer bring us any form of peace or comfort, it would not be terrible of us to move forward without it.

Fix

Every time I prioritized your pain over my own, the message became clearer: I was not obligated to fix you as you were not obligated to fix me. As much as I wanted to help you, I could not continue tending to your needs while neglecting mine, because trying to save you only carved away at my sanity. There was no way for me to be there for you without also feeling pressured to solve your problems; the line between the two had become much too blurry. The more deeply I submerged myself in your burdens, the more challenging it was for me to resurface as the same person I was going in. The truth was I just needed to refrain from trying to be your liberator, and to trust that you would be okay without me. Rejecting that responsibility with which I burdened myself was what freed us both.

Temporary

We try our best to bring certain people along for the whole ride, but they end up staying for only a part of it, and maybe that part is all they are meant for. These people enter our lives to make the journey a little easier, a little more worth embarking, and a lot more doable. It seems reasonable, then, for us to simply forget that they, too, have their own agendas to commit to. We could never ask them to sacrifice what was never their intention to sacrifice, merely to make our ride less bumpy. Sometimes, the right path does not include the people who have led us there, but that should not hinder us from getting to where we need to be. Some people are meant to be temporary in our lives, but what they leave behind does not have to be. Because without them, we would never understand that we deserve permanence and people who are willing to stay for the entire ride.

Fit the Bill

When you are rejected, it will feel like you are the reason things failed to unfold the way you hoped. It will make you think that there are either desirable qualities you lack, or distasteful qualities you possess; nevertheless, believing that either one is true is what will stop you from fully loving yourself. Getting rejected may hurt, but the truth is that it has more to do with the person doing the rejecting than it does with you. Not everyone is for you, as you are not for everyone. If being yourself does not fit the bill, the only thing worse than facing rejection is forcing yourself to be someone you are not and trying to love yourself for it.

Set the Stage

If you give out your love freely but leave none for yourself, you pave the way for others to destroy you. Without any love for yourself, you will always be accepting of whatever you receive, even when it is clear that you deserve more. It is when you are unclear about what you are worthy of that will stand in your way. When you are unaware of what you deserve, you will not be able to recognize sincere love since anything given to you will resemble it. Remember that when you love yourself first, you set the stage for you to be loved right.

Nearly Broken

Holding on to the people who remind us that we are worthy is healing in itself. Sometimes, it takes being with those who have nearly broken us to acknowledge the ones who never would. It is this brokenness that can provoke us to inadvertently push away even the people we need and never want to be without. And maybe we do this because we learned through getting hurt that being alone can sometimes feel safer than being with anyone at all. We can give in to our insecurities as often as we do, but we should not dismiss the people who choose to show up for us, especially when countless others have chosen not to.

Belong

You were always treated in a way that made you feel like good things were not meant for you. Even when they were yours to have, you did not know what to make of them or how to accept them. Anything that involved you that seemed to be heading in the right direction only ended up taking a turn for the worse, which led you to believe that you were hopeless. That others got to define what you deserved. But you never needed the way someone else treated you to determine what you could have in life. You never needed things to pan out first before deciding you could own your happiness. Good things belong to you even when you do not believe you can have them.

Antiseptic

Things that will help us heal may hurt in the beginning, much like the way antiseptic stings on our wounds. It could be the truth we do not want to hear or the act of cutting ties with someone we no longer need in our lives; regardless of what it is, we would be betraying ourselves by holding on to the things that keep us oblivious to the truth or make us feel safe just because it is familiar. Staying with something familiar will always feel more comfortable than moving forward with the unknown. Yet choosing what is comfortable does not mean it is better for us. Adapting to what is better for us will always be challenging if we refuse to accept that it is the better choice. We do not need to hold on to things that make us feel good only some of the time, and we should not be afraid to want something that is good all the time.

Haunted

Dwelling on the past was my favorite pastime. I was always haunted by the way my decisions had hurt other people, even when they seemed like good decisions for me. But this is how life worked. People have to hurt each other because living truthfully in pain is better than living with a false sense of contentment. Being dishonest about one's true feelings to protect the feelings of another does more harm than good for either person. Fixating on things I could have done differently does not change anything now and letting people down easy does not lessen any further pain they might feel. As happy as I want other people to be, I am not responsible for anyone's happiness but my own.

Declutter

Closets and the human heart. Both are filled with things we often need to access, as well as the things we cannot bring ourselves to let go of. When all they do is occupy space and serve as a bittersweet reminder of our past, we are not required to keep them. We are not doing our hearts any favors by continuing to hold on to what no longer has a place in our lives. There are times when it is necessary to declutter—to make room for what matters to us now.

Stay

You can tell yourself you are deserving of love and happiness, but it will not mean much if you have always felt undeserving. You have a tough time believing these things could fall into your lap, so you try to justify the likelihood of it being a mistake whenever a shot at happiness does come along. Anything good that enters your life will seem temporary to you, because you have already painted the picture in your head that good things are not here to stay. The thing is you do not have to *feel* deserving of anything to deserve anything. Your worth is immeasurable regardless of how worthy you feel.

Fighting Chance

No matter how accepting of ourselves we have grown to be, insecurity is something we will deal with again and again. Even when we have done the work to overcome self-doubt, our insecurities have a way of creeping up and stealing moments of joy and growth when we least expect it. When we reveal to others how inadequate we feel, we fear that deep down they might agree with us. We never want to expose our insecurities as that would allow others to tap into our vulnerability, and if we let *that* happen, then we would be setting ourselves up for getting hurt. We do our best to keep them hidden, but not taking control of our insecurities only impedes us from growing out of them. It obstructs us from loving ourselves and others from loving us. If we automatically decide that we cannot be loved, we are not giving ourselves a fighting chance, and that chance is the very least we deserve.

Whole

When you are left with nothing, make sure you are still right with nothing. The presence of another person in your life has always been the metric by which you judge your wholeness, but that should never determine how complete you feel. It is easy to forget that you are whole when you have been repeatedly bent out of shape by those who could not take care of you. But let it sink in that you could never truly break and that you never needed anyone else holding your hand for you to hold yourself up. Even when it feels like pieces of you have been scattered everywhere, they will never be located beyond where you are.

Team

We devote so much to everyone else that we rarely pause to think about ourselves. We forget that our energy and peace are sacred and if ever compromised, we would be losing much more than these parts of us that others never hesitate to take. While giving may be our way of expressing love, it should never be done at the expense of what makes us who we are. Choosing to be on our own team is not a selfish move if choosing others costs us the ability to choose ourselves.

Unsolicited

One belief about love has long been perpetuated: All we want is to love and be loved in return. While we are built for giving and absorbing love, sometimes, and through no fault of our own, the love we willingly give out will be unsolicited. We can offer our love as intensely as we want, but the reality is it will not always be wanted. It does not matter which way we spin it because in the end, we are not in control of how others feel, and nothing good ever transpires from anything forced. So, when they choose not to receive our love, remember that it is equivalent to when we are not receptive to the things we do not want. Our love is not meant for everyone, but in no way does that devalue what we have to offer.

Freedom

You trap yourself when you cannot find it within you to forgive. Maybe you feel that the repercussions of the damage they caused are yours to cope with. That you need to hold on to the pain to validate that you have been hurt. They might always live with the fact that they have hurt you and it may or may not bother them for the rest of their lives, but you do not need to harbor this resentment for the rest of yours. There is freedom in forgiveness. Letting them off the hook lets you off the hook.

Reason

When I feel love, I am totally blinded by it. Love is my reason for ignoring any obvious red flags. It is the reason my pain threshold is so often put to the test. And it is the reason I fully intend to go my way yet always feel more compelled to bend over backwards and go out of my way. But when I feel love, I become the best person I am capable of being. Love is the reason I can see perfection amidst the imperfect. It is the reason I can look past the actions that are sometimes more hurtful than pleasant. It is the reason things I had previously considered to be out of the way are now part of my path.

Heal

All too often, we try to forcibly overcome pain, as if we had control over our feelings. But pain does not disappear by getting ushered out. We must give ourselves what we need to heal, and that includes a place for our pain to stay. A place for it to catch its breath and to figure out how it can best make its exit without hurting us more. Our pain will stay with us for as long as it needs to, and it will leave only when it is ready to.

We will heal only when we are ready to.

Next

I pictured the notion of moving on to look something like going to sleep at night as one person and waking up the next morning as someone entirely different. A different person with different feelings and new insights. But like many of life's underestimated challenges, moving on can only happen when the process is at least somewhat—if not completely— burdensome or painful, and surely not something that happens in the span of one night. If the process of letting go does not hurt you, then could what you are trying to let go of truly have meant much? Moving on is not knowing whether your happiness is guaranteed at the next place you end up going to. It is, however, knowing that wherever you were is certainly not where you want to be again.

Reflection

When they make you feel like there is a part of you that you must suppress, do not discount the possibility that they willed this part of you into existence and are simply in denial of their role. You might feel needy or insecure from time to time, but maybe that is because they have failed to remind you that you are more than enough, wholly worthy of love and attention, and perfect as you are. They will trick you into believing you are the problem, but all you are doing is showing them a reflection of their own inadequacies and inability to love you right.

Two Words

There are times when apologies are tossed in the air like celebratory confetti, when we feel completely unbothered by admitting to being in the wrong. Then, there are the moments when we refuse to apologize because we are too embarrassed to bring ourselves to utter those two words that would jab at our pride. Nobody wants to admit fault, but everybody wants things to magically rectify themselves. When we are able to say, "I'm sorry" and mean it, it may have more to do with wanting to mend a valuable relationship than it does with merely swallowing our pride.

House

We are usually drawn to people for all the right reasons but sometimes stay with them for the wrong ones, then try to justify it with excuses like convenience and familiarity. But when we stay because we have invested every inch of our soul into keeping the house from collapsing, it can be hard to veer away from that feeling of responsibility. Because the house provides us with the only comfort we know and the most that we think we deserve, we continue devoting our time and energy to it and close ourselves off to the idea that there could be something else that is actually worth investing in: ourselves. As uncomfortable as it may be to do so, we can make the difficult choice of choosing ourselves and believing that better things can come from the uncomfortable. Sometimes, we just need to let go of the house and allow it to fall.

Gamble

By choosing to love, you are permitting yourself to get hurt. Apart from the rainbows and butterflies, love is a gamble with plenty at stake. You cannot be selective with what you might get, nor can you decide on love without also being open to the likelihood of being faced with heartache. You will risk a broken heart along the way, but vulnerability is not something you can opt to switch on and off. Love begs you to be vulnerable and to trust that it will bring more light than darkness in your life. Love begs you to take that risk.

Expectations

It was easy to grow frustrated whenever my expectations were unmet. I wanted you to change as much as you wanted to remain the same. But the underlying truth is that people do things willingly only when they want to. I knew when something was a stretch for you even when you had done it anyway, and this was something I was guilty of as well. There were times I pushed myself to do for others what might have been the last things I wanted to do. But what I discovered is that there is greater motivation to do these things when they are done from a place of love. It was from this that I learned a valuable lesson about people which would later help me to accept that even the slightest expectations may not always be fulfilled: I cannot force what does not come naturally, and I cannot be disappointed when nothing comes.

Last Act

We cling so tightly to the assumption that we would be broken if they ever chose to leave us. But being left does not always need to end in tragedy. If love did not afford room for hurting, we would never know healing. Love is not only for the whole hearts; it is tenderly reserved for the ones in pieces. When we are left, we are not left empty-handed. We are left with all that we need to discern what we do not need. If leaving was the last thing they did for us, then it was their last act of love. When people decide to stop wasting our time and energy, that time and energy can be redirected to our own healing and the love we owe ourselves.

Unshackle

I grew up learning that success meant achieving and owning the things I wanted. It had little to do with how I felt about myself or the things I did *not* want. Nobody teaches us that we could suffer from more than just the physical ailments and financial struggles in life. Nobody teaches us how to let go of the people and the worries that constantly bring us unnecessary pain, or even that it matters to let go of such things. We hold on because we do not know better. We learn to carry the weight of everything all on our own, and sometimes, we learn a little too late that success does not always mean accumulating more. It could just mean unshackling the baggage we have been carrying the entire time.

Rock Bottom

Some of us will never know our limits until we hit rock bottom. We tend to test our tolerance by seeing how terribly things can unfold for us before we resort to shaping up or making changes to get to a better place. While being at our lowest point is far from ideal, perhaps we can take momentary comfort in knowing that although we have failed, we most likely did not fail without a fight. Reaching an all-time low just means that we can only rise from there. And seeing as we are often alone on our way to rock bottom, sometimes, our best bet to getting out of such a dark place is none other than ourselves.

The Beauty in Aloneness

A garden of flowers exhibits beauty in its entirety, but a standalone flower does not need to be planted alongside others to grow beautifully. It will flourish like so, regardless of whether or not other flowers are present, and so will we among other people.

Mirror

I was guilty of forgetting. I would forget to remind her that what she brought to the table was always enough. I was guilty of staying silent, of letting her believe that she had to be more than what she was if she wanted to be worthy. I held the power to change her life and did not know this until I stood in front of the mirror and saw that we both had the same apologetic look on our faces. It was the look of hopelessness and doubt. I told her I did not mean to let her down. I told her I have always believed that she was enough, and that was all she needed to hear.

Shed

There were nights they did not come home. Times when they stormed out, which left us brooding over the possibility that the relationship had ended. Our thoughts and feelings were dismissed long before they were given a chance to be communicated. All of these moments have hurt us, but the pain has strengthened us in more ways than it has debilitated us. We grew more resilient when we did not think we could be any stronger. We learned that making light of our feelings only reinforced the way they treated us. It was through struggling with this pain that we figured out what we needed and, more importantly, what could be shed.

Permission

When I was heartbroken, I believed that I was not allowed to move on from the pain because of the delusion that I had done something to deserve it. Sometimes we attribute the guilt to ourselves when things fall apart, which then has us convinced that we should suffer as punishment. We insist on staying hurt as a way of reinforcing and validating our guilt, almost as if to redeem ourselves by it. But even when we feel responsible for how things turned out, choosing pain as punishment is not the way to heal. By believing we are not allowed to overcome this guilt, we will never be able to move past the pain. Only when we give ourselves the permission to heal can we begin to move forward.

Enough

Maybe all we want is somebody in our corner. Somebody who will not do the work for us, but rather be our greatest supporter as we reach our greatest goals. Somebody who will not abandon ship the instant they are affected by the things that affect us. Maybe we want somebody who will never do things for us out of obligation or gallantry. Maybe we want somebody who just wants to be there for every moment of our journey to let us know we are not alone. Sometimes, that is enough.

React

When someone hurts you and you lash out in defense, you might regret it afterward and aim to apologize for overreacting. But in the process, you might make the mistake of apologizing for feeling hurt, which would overall be far worse than choosing not to apologize for the way you reacted. Maybe you can overlook it but dismissing your honest feelings will only show to others how little you consider your worth to be. If you are going to be sorry for anything, make sure it is not for the way they made you feel.

Mistaken

We all want to be right because being right feels good and empowers us with a sense of strength we can stand tall behind. Or maybe it is that we would rather not be wrong, because being wrong would put us in a vulnerable position. We find it easier to apologize for our actions when they say nothing about who we are. It is when we cannot separate the action from our character that makes being wrong more difficult to acknowledge. Without that clear distinction, we may feel like the world is merely waiting for us to admit that there is something wrong with us. But we can be mistaken and still embrace when we are wrong without letting our mistakes define us.

Reclaim

Despite what you do, people will inevitably judge you. They decide who you are even when their opinion of you may be completely off-base, and sadly not much can be done about it. It is when they find a way to get under your skin, knowing that you care so much about what they think, that you give away your power. They know what they mean to you and because of that, they know you will do what you can to please them—and you would do anything if that meant *you* meant something to them. When you finally realize that yielding to their manipulation of you is only tearing you down, understand that the only way to escape it is by reclaiming your power. Setting boundaries for yourself is one thing but honoring them is another. If you never honor your boundaries, you will always condone being mistreated by those who do not mind it.

Last Drop

While constantly giving can be taxing, it, more than anything, brings me joy. And because it brings me joy, I always find ways to pour from my cup even when I am nearing my last drop. I have given when there was nothing to gain, and even at times when there was something to lose. When you find yourself regularly showing up for others, it becomes harder to determine when enough is enough. Giving might be your greatest source of vitality and fulfillment, but you cannot give what you do not have. It will be difficult but once you put a cap on how much you give to others, you will avoid giving away the love reserved for you.

Return

We often try to be mindful of how we make others feel, but it is impossible to spare everyone from getting their feelings hurt. Knowing full well that we can cause people suffering, we are still going to make the choices that could hurt them as we continue discovering who we want to be. When living our truth comes as a disappointment to some, we may find ourselves plagued with guilt. It is when we allow this guilt to make us feel like bad people that we happen to lose our way. By not veering from what is true to the heart, however, is how we return to ourselves. The things we do on the path toward our truth will not please everyone and that does not make us bad people.

Miracle

Change that is underway will not always be noticeable, but that is of course if we choose to close our eyes to it. We will never be able to acknowledge any progress if we are already convinced that none of it will happen. Too often we grow disappointed when we fail to see the transformation we have concocted in our heads, when really, we were simply refusing to believe it was even possible to begin with. Sometimes, the miracle is in trusting the process. Giving change a chance to happen is only the first part of it.

Hand in Hand

Maybe all we have ever done is try to close the door on heartache, forgetting that it tags along with the love we welcome so warmly. We treat love and heartache as separate entities, denying that the two go hand in hand. We nurture this idea that being loved means never getting hurt and that if we ever did get hurt, then the love must come to an end. But forgiveness and healing require that we hurt first. We could never hope to grow from our moments of pain if we limit ourselves to thinking that love comprises only the good and easy parts.

Constant

My heart frequently took the blame for things it was never at fault for. I reprimanded it for being too weak, too passive, and too trusting, when in fact there is nothing about it that I would change. I never thanked it for holding me together when I felt myself falling apart, and for all the times it guided me out of broken places unscathed. It is what allowed me to remain soft when all I wanted was to harden, grow cold, and turn away from the world. My heart has been my constant throughout the times the people I relied on had not been.

Giver

You are a giver. No matter the cost, you will find it within you to keep on providing for others if that is what will keep them from sinking. When you fail to assert your boundaries, you assume the title of giver—and takers know this. Takers do not care if you are in the right headspace, so they will go so far as to rob you of your peace if you simply allow it. Every time you put the needs of others first, you miss any opportunity to think about your own. While helping others to stay afloat is easily what you do, it is also exactly how you end up overlooking the holes at the bottom of your boat.

Fair Chance

If you are rushing to heal, you are cutting corners to get to a place that can be reached only with time. Forcing yourself to feel a certain way when you have not even taken the time to process your feelings will cause you to be out of tune with where you truly are in your healing. Growing from what has hurt you requires courage but also your discomfort; it requires that you sit with your pain and feel through it before anything else. Learning from past mistakes would be impossible to do if every step forward was painless and within your comfort zone. Your life is not guaranteed to be any better or easier after you have healed, but at least you would be giving yourself a fair chance at having that life by putting in the work to get there.

Duty

Our duty to ourselves is to let nothing and no one compromise the light within us. People will try to destroy our light when they feel excluded from our journey or when they are unable to travel down the same path as us. But that does not mean we reduce ourselves for the comfort of those we would rather not hurt or disappoint. We do not dim our light simply because what they have to offer does not parallel what we bring to the table. We can shine while being mindful of not blinding others in the process. To sacrifice our light is to abandon our truth, and the occurrence of either would be largely instrumental in losing ourselves entirely.

Roots

Choosing to move on means every fraction of us has to commit. It does not happen if even a small part of us is still holding on to—practically safeguarding—the hurt. We move on only when our entire being can let go of what has been keeping us rooted in a place of pain. I was guilty of taking these roots with me wherever I found myself heading to next, not realizing I was subtly trying to find new, snug spots in which I could replant them. But things we take from the past never truly have a permanent place in the present. All they do is get in the way of what we genuinely seek on our journey. So, if there is anything we should be taking from the past, let it be the lessons learned.

Green Light

Loving yourself does not mean accepting inconsistent love whenever it is conveniently offered. It does not mean allowing yourself to be exploited in order to please others and be liked by them. Loving yourself means sometimes having to do the hardest thing imaginable: saying no. Saying no is hard because it can take every ounce of you to resist giving in to them. It is hard because you know it would be much easier to accept their recycled apology, and then pretend that the way they hurt you made absolutely no impact on your life. If you do not stand up for yourself, you are telling your heart that it is okay for it to take the beating. You are giving others the green light to continue giving you the same treatment you always told yourself you would never tolerate. While they may never comprehend that they can hurt others, it is not your responsibility to suffer the consequences of their negligent choices.

Remedy

We have all been there. We have all felt the type of pain that led us to other people. The type of pain that told us we would find solutions only by looking to other people for them. We hold ludicrous expectations that others will somehow provide the relief we need or have the answers to our problems. Holding others responsible for making us feel better seems like the ideal and easy way to get rid of our pain, but sometimes, we can cause ourselves to hurt even further just by having these hopes and insisting on answers we may never receive. Even if we are not the reason for our suffering, it is not up to others to remedy it. What we fail to realize most of the time is that the remedy for our pain has been there all along—we are the very solution we continually seek in others yet will only find in ourselves.